AVOIDANT ATTACHMENT WORKBOOK

Cognitive Behavioral Therapy Worksheets for Those Recovering From Avoidant Attachment Style

**BY
DARIO JEYCO**
COPYRIGHT © 2023

EXPOSURE THERAPY
FOR
EMOTIONAL CLOSENESS

Individuals with avoidant attachment may struggle to get close to others, feel unworthy of love and even more so fear getting hurt.

They may avoid emotional intimacy or physical touch, because they see this as threatening.

Start small by engaging in low-risk, casual interactions with others.

This could mean saying hello to a neighbor or coworker, or having a brief conversation with a stranger.

Gradually increase the level of intimacy over time.

	TASK ACCOMPLISHED ☐ intimacy level ○○○○○
	TASK ACCOMPLISHED ☐ intimacy level ○○○○○
	TASK ACCOMPLISHED ☐ intimacy level ○○○○○

NOTES

....

....

OVERCOMING AVOIDANT ATTACHMENT WORKSHEET

This table will help you to study the effect of the repercussions of the anxious avoidant attachment style in your social interactions on a daily, weekly or monthly basis... The aim of this paper is to develop an appropriate coping plan to control the negative signs if you want to make a real change in your personality.

AVOIDANT ATTACHMENT TAGS AND TRAITS	What are the traits of avoidant attachment style that you experienced today? Describe how this affected your dealings.
	👍 **WHAT WAS SO COOL:** ✋ **WHAT WAS WRONG:**

AVOIDANT ATTACHMENT WORKSHEET -DBT-

Date: / /

Sleep Quality :

START YOUR DAY MINDFULLY WITH A FEW MINUTES OF MEDITATION OR MINDFULNESS. THIS PRACTICE WILL HELP YOU FEEL CENTERED, ENHANCE SELF-AWARENESS, AND ESTABLISH A POSITIVE MINDSET FOR THE DAY.

TAKE A MOMENT TO REFLECT ON YOUR EMOTIONS AND EMOTIONAL STATE. ASK YOURSELF ABOUT YOUR FEELINGS, THOUGHTS, AND ANY ATTACHMENT-RELATED PATTERNS YOU MIGHT OBSERVE.

EMBRACE POSITIVE AFFIRMATIONS THAT FOSTER TRUST, VULNERABILITY, AND EMOTIONAL CONNECTION. REPEAT PHRASES LIKE 'I AM DESERVING OF LOVE AND CONNECTION,' 'I AM OPEN TO EMOTIONAL INTIMACY,' OR 'I CAN CONFIDE IN OTHERS WITH MY FEELINGS.'

✓ ___ : ___

✓ ___ : ___

Daily Wins

Mood Tracking ✓

ANGRY	☐
ANNOYED	☐
ANXIOUS	☐
ASHAMED	☐
EMBARRASSING	☐
COURAGEOUS	☐
CALM	☐
CHEERFUL	☐
COLD	☐
CONFUSED	☐
DISCOURAGED	☐
DISTRACTED	☐
EMBARRASSED	☐
EXCITED	☐
FRIENDLY	☐
GUILTY	☐
HAPPY	☐
HOPEFUL	☐
SOLITARY	☐
BELOVED	☐
NERVOUS	☐
OFFENDED	☐
AFRAID	☐
THOUGHTFUL	☐
TIRED OUT	☐
UNCOMFORTABLE	☐
UNCERTAIN	☐

DAILY MOOD CYCLE

Instructions: Think about your day from start to finish. Color the first square to express your feelings each time of the day. Next, write a word that reflects your feelings, and draw in the circle a picture of your face that reflects your feelings at that moment.

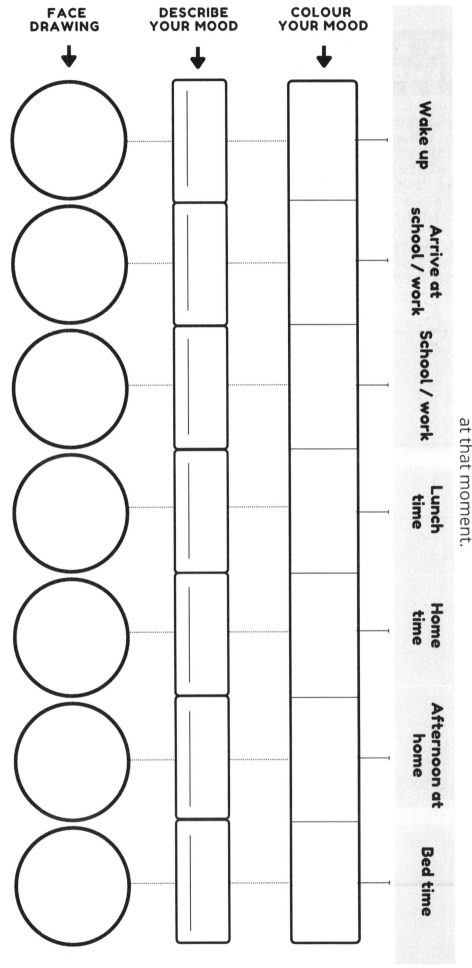

FACE DRAWING

DESCRIBE YOUR MOOD

COLOUR YOUR MOOD

- Wake up
- Arrive at school / work
- School / work
- Lunch time
- Home time
- Afternoon at home
- Bed time

AVOIDANT ATTACHMENT WORKSHEET

Date : _____

DAILY / WEEKLY - DBT WORKSHEET (OPTIONAL)

- List three emotions that surfaced throughout yesterday. Reflect on how each emotion affected my interactions and decisions.
- Write a kind and supportive message to myself, focusing on self-acceptance and understanding.
- What are the prospects that will make you give up the difficulty of trusting others and open up.
- Write down one boundary I can set today to prioritize my emotional well-being.
- Write down any lingering worries or thoughts before bedtime, and consider ways to ease them.

Everything related to changing your beliefs about refusing to allow others to approach you for fear of rejection.

_____

_____

_____

_____

_____

_____

_____

_____

_____

_____

_____

_____

_____

_____

_____

DATE :   /   /

EXPOSURE THERAPY
FOR
EMOTIONAL CLOSENESS

Individuals with avoidant attachment may struggle to get close to others, feel unworthy of love and even more so fear getting hurt.

They may avoid emotional intimacy or physical touch, because they see this as threatening.

Start small by engaging in low-risk, casual interactions with others.

This could mean saying hello to a neighbor or coworker, or having a brief conversation with a stranger.

Gradually increase the level of intimacy over time.

	TASK ACCOMPLISHED ☐ intimacy level ○ ○ ○ ○ ○
	TASK ACCOMPLISHED ☐ intimacy level ○ ○ ○ ○ ○
	TASK ACCOMPLISHED ☐ intimacy level ○ ○ ○ ○ ○

NOTES

....

....

OVERCOMING AVOIDANT ATTACHMENT WORKSHEET

This table will help you to study the effect of the repercussions of the anxious avoidant attachment style in your social interactions on a daily, weekly or monthly basis... The aim of this paper is to develop an appropriate coping plan to control the negative signs if you want to make a real change in your personality.

AVOIDANT ATTACHMENT TAGS AND TRAITS	What are the traits of avoidant attachment style that you experienced today? Describe how this affected your dealings.
	👍 WHAT WAS SO COOL: ✋ WHAT WAS WRONG:

AVOIDANT ATTACHMENT WORKSHEET -DBT-

START YOUR DAY MINDFULLY WITH A FEW MINUTES OF MEDITATION OR MINDFULNESS. THIS PRACTICE WILL HELP YOU FEEL CENTERED, ENHANCE SELF-AWARENESS, AND ESTABLISH A POSITIVE MINDSET FOR THE DAY.
TAKE A MOMENT TO REFLECT ON YOUR EMOTIONS AND EMOTIONAL STATE. ASK YOURSELF ABOUT YOUR FEELINGS, THOUGHTS, AND ANY ATTACHMENT-RELATED PATTERNS YOU MIGHT OBSERVE.
EMBRACE POSITIVE AFFIRMATIONS THAT FOSTER TRUST, VULNERABILITY, AND EMOTIONAL CONNECTION. REPEAT PHRASES LIKE "I AM DESERVING OF LOVE AND CONNECTION," "I AM OPEN TO EMOTIONAL INTIMACY," OR "I CAN CONFIDE IN OTHERS WITH MY FEELINGS."

✓ ___ : ___

✓ ___ : ___

Daily Wins

Date: / /

Sleep Quality :

Mood Tracking ✓

Mood	
ANGRY	☐
ANNOYED	☐
ANXIOUS	☐
ASHAMED	☐
EMBARRASSING	☐
COURAGEOUS	☐
CALM	☐
CHEERFUL	☐
COLD	☐
CONFUSED	☐
DISCOURAGED	☐
DISTRACTED	☐
EMBARRASSED	☐
EXCITED	☐
FRIENDLY	☐
GUILTY	☐
HAPPY	☐
HOPEFUL	☐
SOLITARY	☐
BELOVED	☐
NERVOUS	☐
OFFENDED	☐
AFRAID	☐
THOUGHTFUL	☐
TIRED OUT	☐
UNCOMFORTABLE	☐
UNCERTAIN	☐

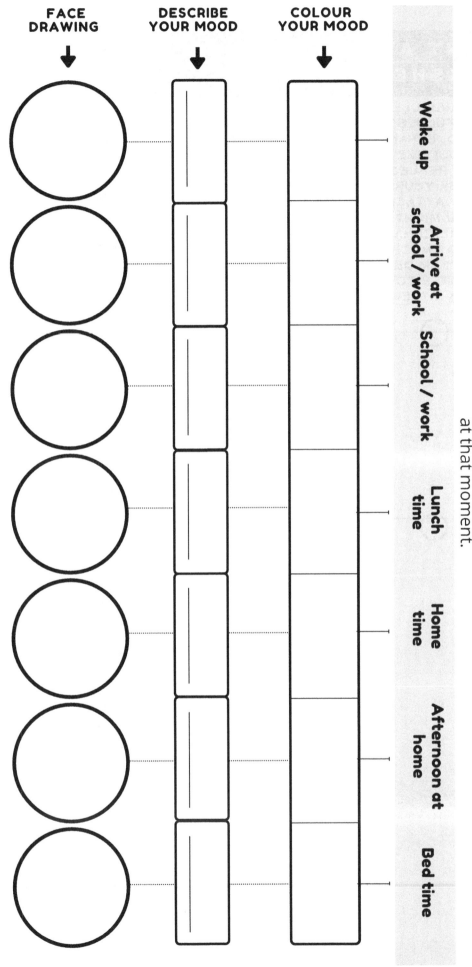

DAILY MOOD CYCLE

Instructions: Think about your day from start to finish. Color the first square to express your feelings each time of the day. Next, write a word that reflects your feelings, and draw in the circle a picture of your face that reflects your feelings at that moment.

FACE DRAWING

DESCRIBE YOUR MOOD

COLOUR YOUR MOOD

Wake up

Arrive at school / work

School / work

Lunch time

Home time

Afternoon at home

Bed time

AVOIDANT ATTACHMENT WORKSHEET

Date : _____

DAILY / WEEKLY - DBT WORKSHEET (OPTIONAL)

- List three emotions that surfaced throughout yesterday. Reflect on how each emotion affected my interactions and decisions.
- Write a kind and supportive message to myself, focusing on self-acceptance and understanding.
- What are the prospects that will make you give up the difficulty of trusting others and open up.
- Write down one boundary I can set today to prioritize my emotional well-being.
- Write down any lingering worries or thoughts before bedtime, and consider ways to ease them.

Everything related to changing your beliefs about refusing to allow others to approach you for fear of rejection.

_____

_____

_____

_____

_____

_____

_____

_____

_____

_____

_____

_____

_____

_____

_____

DATE :   /   /

EXPOSURE THERAPY
FOR
EMOTIONAL CLOSENESS

Individuals with avoidant attachment may struggle to get close to others, feel unworthy of love and even more so fear getting hurt.

They may avoid emotional intimacy or physical touch, because they see this as threatening.

Start small by engaging in low-risk, casual interactions with others.

This could mean saying hello to a neighbor or coworker, or having a brief conversation with a stranger.

Gradually increase the level of intimacy over time.

	TASK ACCOMPLISHED □ intimacy level ○ ○ ○ ○ ○
	TASK ACCOMPLISHED □ intimacy level ○ ○ ○ ○ ○
	TASK ACCOMPLISHED □ intimacy level ○ ○ ○ ○ ○

NOTES

....

....

OVERCOMING AVOIDANT ATTACHMENT WORKSHEET

This table will help you to study the effect of the repercussions of the anxious avoidant attachment style in your social interactions on a daily, weekly or monthly basis... The aim of this paper is to develop an appropriate coping plan to control the negative signs if you want to make a real change in your personality.

AVOIDANT ATTACHMENT TAGS AND TRAITS	What are the traits of avoidant attachment style that you experienced today? Describe how this affected your dealings.
	👍 WHAT WAS SO COOL: 🖐 WHAT WAS WRONG:

AVOIDANT ATTACHMENT WORKSHEET -DBT-

START YOUR DAY MINDFULLY WITH A FEW MINUTES OF
MEDITATION OR MINDFULNESS. THIS PRACTICE WILL HELP
YOU FEEL CENTERED, ENHANCE SELF-AWARENESS, AND
ESTABLISH A POSITIVE MINDSET FOR THE DAY.
TAKE A MOMENT TO REFLECT ON YOUR EMOTIONS AND
EMOTIONAL STATE. ASK YOURSELF ABOUT YOUR FEELINGS,
THOUGHTS, AND ANY ATTACHMENT-RELATED PATTERNS
YOU MIGHT OBSERVE.
EMBRACE POSITIVE AFFIRMATIONS THAT FOSTER TRUST,
VULNERABILITY, AND EMOTIONAL CONNECTION. REPEAT
PHRASES LIKE "I AM DESERVING OF LOVE AND
CONNECTION," "I AM OPEN TO EMOTIONAL INTIMACY," OR "I
CAN CONFIDE IN OTHERS WITH MY FEELINGS."

___ : ___

___ : ___

Daily Wins

Mood Tracking

ANGRY	☐
ANNOYED	☐
ANXIOUS	☐
ASHAMED	☐
EMBARRASSING	☐
COURAGEOUS	☐
CALM	☐
CHEERFUL	☐
COLD	☐
CONFUSED	☐
DISCOURAGED	☐
DISTRACTED	☐
EMBARRASSED	☐
EXCITED	☐
FRIENDLY	☐
GUILTY	☐
HAPPY	☐
HOPEFUL	☐
SOLITARY	☐
BELOVED	☐
NERVOUS	☐
OFFENDED	☐
AFRAID	☐
THOUGHTFUL	☐
TIRED OUT	☐
UNCOMFORTABLE	☐
UNCERTAIN	☐

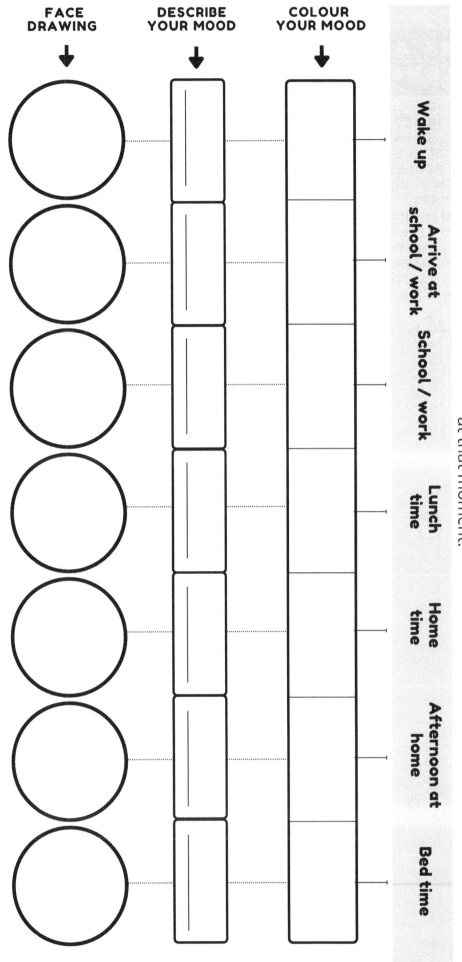

DAILY MOOD CYCLE

Instructions: Think about your day from start to finish. Color the first square to express your feelings each time of the day. Next, write a word that reflects your feelings, and draw in the circle a picture of your face that reflects your feelings at that moment.

FACE DRAWING

DESCRIBE YOUR MOOD

COLOUR YOUR MOOD

Wake up

Arrive at school / work

School / work

Lunch time

Home time

Afternoon at home

Bed time

AVOIDANT ATTACHMENT WORKSHEET

Date : _____

DAILY / WEEKLY - DBT WORKSHEET (OPTIONAL)

- List three emotions that surfaced throughout yesterday. Reflect on how each emotion affected my interactions and decisions.
- Write a kind and supportive message to myself, focusing on self-acceptance and understanding.
- What are the prospects that will make you give up the difficulty of trusting others and open up.
- Write down one boundary I can set today to prioritize my emotional well-being.
- Write down any lingering worries or thoughts before bedtime, and consider ways to ease them.

Everything related to changing your beliefs about refusing to allow others to approach you for fear of rejection.

_____

_____

_____

_____

_____

_____

_____

_____

_____

_____

_____

_____

_____

_____

DATE :   /   /

EXPOSURE THERAPY FOR EMOTIONAL CLOSENESS

Individuals with avoidant attachment may struggle to get close to others, feel unworthy of love and even more so fear getting hurt.

They may avoid emotional intimacy or physical touch, because they see this as threatening.

Start small by engaging in low-risk, casual interactions with others.

This could mean saying hello to a neighbor or coworker, or having a brief conversation with a stranger.

Gradually increase the level of intimacy over time.

	TASK ACCOMPLISHED ☐ intimacy level ○ ○ ○ ○ ○
	TASK ACCOMPLISHED ☐ intimacy level ○ ○ ○ ○ ○
	TASK ACCOMPLISHED ☐ intimacy level ○ ○ ○ ○ ○

NOTES

....

....

OVERCOMING AVOIDANT ATTACHMENT WORKSHEET

This table will help you to study the effect of the repercussions of the anxious avoidant attachment style in your social interactions on a daily, weekly or monthly basis... The aim of this paper is to develop an appropriate coping plan to control the negative signs if you want to make a real change in your personality.

AVOIDANT ATTACHMENT TAGS AND TRAITS	What are the traits of avoidant attachment style that you experienced today? Describe how this affected your dealings.
	👍 WHAT WAS SO COOL: ✋ WHAT WAS WRONG:

AVOIDANT ATTACHMENT WORKSHEET -DBT-

START YOUR DAY MINDFULLY WITH A FEW MINUTES OF MEDITATION OR MINDFULNESS. THIS PRACTICE WILL HELP YOU FEEL CENTERED, ENHANCE SELF-AWARENESS, AND ESTABLISH A POSITIVE MINDSET FOR THE DAY.
TAKE A MOMENT TO REFLECT ON YOUR EMOTIONS AND EMOTIONAL STATE. ASK YOURSELF ABOUT YOUR FEELINGS, THOUGHTS, AND ANY ATTACHMENT-RELATED PATTERNS YOU MIGHT OBSERVE.
EMBRACE POSITIVE AFFIRMATIONS THAT FOSTER TRUST, VULNERABILITY, AND EMOTIONAL CONNECTION. REPEAT PHRASES LIKE "I AM DESERVING OF LOVE AND CONNECTION," "I AM OPEN TO EMOTIONAL INTIMACY," OR "I CAN CONFIDE IN OTHERS WITH MY FEELINGS."

Mood Tracking ✔

- ANGRY ☐
- ANNOYED ☐
- ANXIOUS ☐
- ASHAMED ☐
- EMBARRASSING ☐
- COURAGEOUS ☐
- CALM ☐
- CHEERFUL ☐
- COLD ☐
- CONFUSED ☐
- DISCOURAGED ☐
- DISTRACTED ☐
- EMBARRASSED ☐
- EXCITED ☐
- FRIENDLY ☐
- GUILTY ☐
- HAPPY ☐
- HOPEFUL ☐
- SOLITARY ☐
- BELOVED ☐
- NERVOUS ☐
- OFFENDED ☐
- AFRAID ☐
- THOUGHTFUL ☐
- TIRED OUT ☐
- UNCOMFORTABLE ☐
- UNCERTAIN ☐

Daily Wins

DAILY MOOD CYCLE

Instructions: Think about your day from start to finish. Color the first square to express your feelings each time of the day. Next, write a word that reflects your feelings, and draw in the circle a picture of your face that reflects your feelings at that moment.

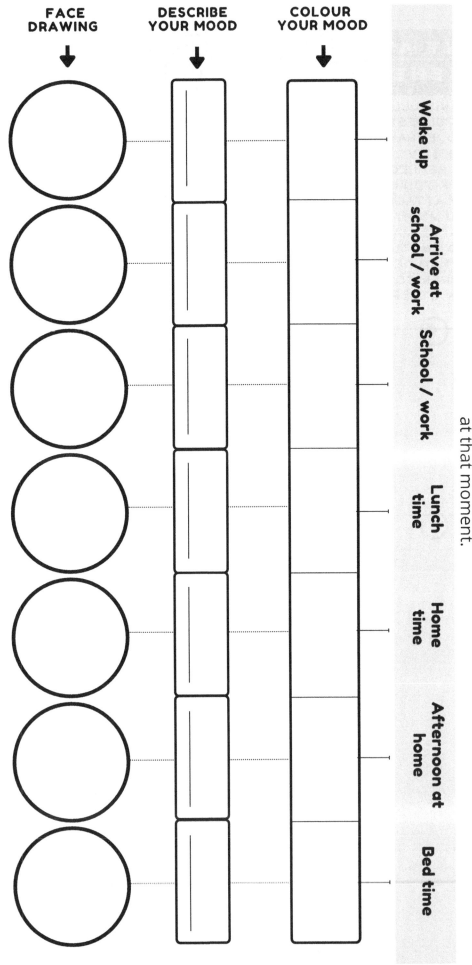

FACE DRAWING

DESCRIBE YOUR MOOD

COLOUR YOUR MOOD

Wake up

Arrive at school / work

School / work

Lunch time

Home time

Afternoon at home

Bed time

AVOIDANT ATTACHMENT WORKSHEET

Date : _____

DAILY / WEEKLY - DBT WORKSHEET (OPTIONAL)

- List three emotions that surfaced throughout yesterday. Reflect on how each emotion affected my interactions and decisions.
- Write a kind and supportive message to myself, focusing on self-acceptance and understanding.
- What are the prospects that will make you give up the difficulty of trusting others and open up.
- Write down one boundary I can set today to prioritize my emotional well-being.
- Write down any lingering worries or thoughts before bedtime, and consider ways to ease them.

Everything related to changing your beliefs about refusing to allow others to approach you for fear of rejection.

_____

_____

_____

_____

_____

_____

_____

_____

_____

_____

_____

_____

_____

_____

_____

_____

DATE :   /   /

EXPOSURE THERAPY
FOR
EMOTIONAL CLOSENESS

Individuals with avoidant attachment may struggle to get close to others, feel unworthy of love and even more so fear getting hurt.

They may avoid emotional intimacy or physical touch, because they see this as threatening.

Start small by engaging in low-risk, casual interactions with others.

This could mean saying hello to a neighbor or coworker, or having a brief conversation with a stranger.

Gradually increase the level of intimacy over time.

	TASK ACCOMPLISHED ☐ intimacy level ○ ○ ○ ○ ○
	TASK ACCOMPLISHED ☐ intimacy level ○ ○ ○ ○ ○
	TASK ACCOMPLISHED ☐ intimacy level ○ ○ ○ ○ ○

NOTES

....

....

OVERCOMING AVOIDANT ATTACHMENT WORKSHEET

This table will help you to study the effect of the repercussions of the anxious avoidant attachment style in your social interactions on a daily, weekly or monthly basis... The aim of this paper is to develop an appropriate coping plan to control the negative signs if you want to make a real change in your personality.

AVOIDANT ATTACHMENT TAGS AND TRAITS	What are the traits of avoidant attachment style that you experienced today? Describe how this affected your dealings.
	👍 WHAT WAS SO COOL: ✋ WHAT WAS WRONG:

AVOIDANT ATTACHMENT WORKSHEET -DBT-

START YOUR DAY MINDFULLY WITH A FEW MINUTES OF MEDITATION OR MINDFULNESS. THIS PRACTICE WILL HELP YOU FEEL CENTERED, ENHANCE SELF-AWARENESS, AND ESTABLISH A POSITIVE MINDSET FOR THE DAY.
TAKE A MOMENT TO REFLECT ON YOUR EMOTIONS AND EMOTIONAL STATE. ASK YOURSELF ABOUT YOUR FEELINGS, THOUGHTS, AND ANY ATTACHMENT-RELATED PATTERNS YOU MIGHT OBSERVE.
EMBRACE POSITIVE AFFIRMATIONS THAT FOSTER TRUST, VULNERABILITY, AND EMOTIONAL CONNECTION. REPEAT PHRASES LIKE "I AM DESERVING OF LOVE AND CONNECTION," "I AM OPEN TO EMOTIONAL INTIMACY," OR "I CAN CONFIDE IN OTHERS WITH MY FEELINGS."

Ⓥ ___ : ___

Ⓥ ___ : ___

Daily Wins

Mood Tracking ✓

Mood	
ANGRY	☐
ANNOYED	☐
ANXIOUS	☐
ASHAMED	☐
EMBARRASSING	☐
COURAGEOUS	☐
CALM	☐
CHEERFUL	☐
COLD	☐
CONFUSED	☐
DISCOURAGED	☐
DISTRACTED	☐
EMBARRASSED	☐
EXCITED	☐
FRIENDLY	☐
GUILTY	☐
HAPPY	☐
HOPEFUL	☐
SOLITARY	☐
BELOVED	☐
NERVOUS	☐
OFFENDED	☐
AFRAID	☐
THOUGHTFUL	☐
TIRED OUT	☐
UNCOMFORTABLE	☐
UNCERTAIN	☐

DAILY MOOD CYCLE

Instructions: Think about your day from start to finish. Color the first square to express your feelings each time of the day. Next, write a word that reflects your feelings, and draw in the circle a picture of your face that reflects your feelings at that moment.

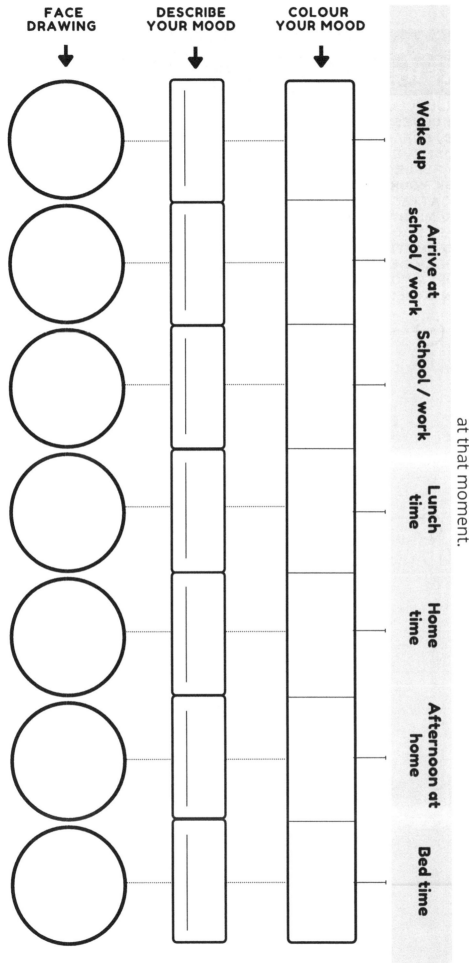

FACE DRAWING

DESCRIBE YOUR MOOD

COLOUR YOUR MOOD

- Wake up
- Arrive at school / work
- School / work
- Lunch time
- Home time
- Afternoon at home
- Bed time

AVOIDANT ATTACHMENT WORKSHEET

Date : _____

DAILY / WEEKLY - DBT WORKSHEET (OPTIONAL)

- List three emotions that surfaced throughout yesterday. Reflect on how each emotion affected my interactions and decisions.
- Write a kind and supportive message to myself, focusing on self-acceptance and understanding.
- What are the prospects that will make you give up the difficulty of trusting others and open up.
- Write down one boundary I can set today to prioritize my emotional well-being.
- Write down any lingering worries or thoughts before bedtime, and consider ways to ease them.

Everything related to changing your beliefs about refusing to allow others to approach you for fear of rejection.

_____

_____

_____

_____

_____

_____

_____

_____

_____

_____

_____

_____

_____

_____

_____

DATE :   /   /

EXPOSURE THERAPY
FOR
EMOTIONAL CLOSENESS

Individuals with avoidant attachment may struggle to get close to others, feel unworthy of love and even more so fear getting hurt.
   They may avoid emotional intimacy or physical touch, because they see this as threatening.
Start small by engaging in low-risk, casual interactions with others.
This could mean saying hello to a neighbor or coworker, or having a brief conversation with a stranger.
Gradually increase the level of intimacy over time.

	TASK ACCOMPLISHED □ intimacy level ○ ○ ○ ○ ○
	TASK ACCOMPLISHED □ intimacy level ○ ○ ○ ○ ○
	TASK ACCOMPLISHED □ intimacy level ○ ○ ○ ○ ○

NOTES

....

....

DATE :   /   /

OVERCOMING AVOIDANT ATTACHMENT WORKSHEET

This table will help you to study the effect of the repercussions of the anxious avoidant attachment style in your social interactions on a daily, weekly or monthly basis... The aim of this paper is to develop an appropriate coping plan to control the negative signs if you want to make a real change in your personality.

AVOIDANT ATTACHMENT TAGS AND TRAITS	What are the traits of avoidant attachment style that you experienced today? Describe how this affected your dealings.
	👍 WHAT WAS SO COOL: ✋ WHAT WAS WRONG:

AVOIDANT ATTACHMENT WORKSHEET -DBT-

START YOUR DAY MINDFULLY WITH A FEW MINUTES OF MEDITATION OR MINDFULNESS. THIS PRACTICE WILL HELP YOU FEEL CENTERED, ENHANCE SELF-AWARENESS, AND ESTABLISH A POSITIVE MINDSET FOR THE DAY.
TAKE A MOMENT TO REFLECT ON YOUR EMOTIONS AND EMOTIONAL STATE. ASK YOURSELF ABOUT YOUR FEELINGS, THOUGHTS, AND ANY ATTACHMENT-RELATED PATTERNS YOU MIGHT OBSERVE.
EMBRACE POSITIVE AFFIRMATIONS THAT FOSTER TRUST, VULNERABILITY, AND EMOTIONAL CONNECTION. REPEAT PHRASES LIKE "I AM DESERVING OF LOVE AND CONNECTION," "I AM OPEN TO EMOTIONAL INTIMACY," OR "I CAN CONFIDE IN OTHERS WITH MY FEELINGS."

✅ ___ : ___

✅ ___ : ___

Daily Wins

Mood Tracking ✔

Mood	
ANGRY	☐
ANNOYED	☐
ANXIOUS	☐
ASHAMED	☐
EMBARRASSING	☐
COURAGEOUS	☐
CALM	☐
CHEERFUL	☐
COLD	☐
CONFUSED	☐
DISCOURAGED	☐
DISTRACTED	☐
EMBARRASSED	☐
EXCITED	☐
FRIENDLY	☐
GUILTY	☐
HAPPY	☐
HOPEFUL	☐
SOLITARY	☐
BELOVED	☐
NERVOUS	☐
OFFENDED	☐
AFRAID	☐
THOUGHTFUL	☐
TIRED OUT	☐
UNCOMFORTABLE	☐
UNCERTAIN	☐

DAILY MOOD CYCLE

Instructions: Think about your day from start to finish. Color the first square to express your feelings each time of the day. Next, write a word that reflects your feelings, and draw in the circle a picture of your face that reflects your feelings at that moment.

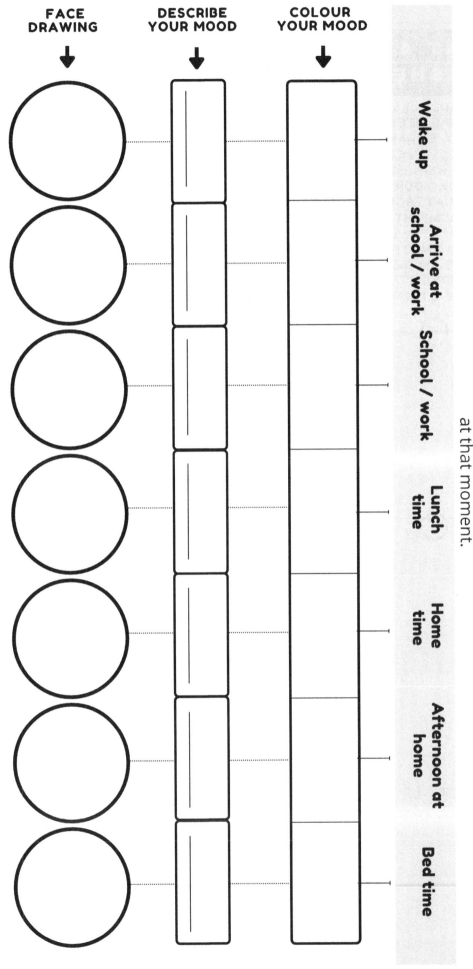

FACE DRAWING

DESCRIBE YOUR MOOD

COLOUR YOUR MOOD

Wake up

Arrive at school / work

School / work

Lunch time

Home time

Afternoon at home

Bed time

AVOIDANT ATTACHMENT WORKSHEET

Date : _____

DAILY / WEEKLY - DBT WORKSHEET (OPTIONAL)

- List three emotions that surfaced throughout yesterday. Reflect on how each emotion affected my interactions and decisions.
- Write a kind and supportive message to myself, focusing on self-acceptance and understanding.
- What are the prospects that will make you give up the difficulty of trusting others and open up.
- Write down one boundary I can set today to prioritize my emotional well-being.
- Write down any lingering worries or thoughts before bedtime, and consider ways to ease them.

Everything related to changing your beliefs about refusing to allow others to approach you for fear of rejection.

_____

_____

_____

_____

_____

_____

_____

_____

_____

_____

_____

_____

_____

_____

_____

DATE :   /   /

EXPOSURE THERAPY
FOR
EMOTIONAL CLOSENESS

Individuals with avoidant attachment may struggle to get close to others, feel unworthy of love and even more so fear getting hurt.

They may avoid emotional intimacy or physical touch, because they see this as threatening.

Start small by engaging in low-risk, casual interactions with others.

This could mean saying hello to a neighbor or coworker, or having a brief conversation with a stranger.

Gradually increase the level of intimacy over time.

	TASK ACCOMPLISHED ☐ intimacy level ○ ○ ○ ○ ○
	TASK ACCOMPLISHED ☐ intimacy level ○ ○ ○ ○ ○
	TASK ACCOMPLISHED ☐ intimacy level ○ ○ ○ ○ ○

NOTES

....

....

OVERCOMING AVOIDANT ATTACHMENT WORKSHEET

This table will help you to study the effect of the repercussions of the anxious avoidant attachment style in your social interactions on a daily, weekly or monthly basis... The aim of this paper is to develop an appropriate coping plan to control the negative signs if you want to make a real change in your personality.

AVOIDANT ATTACHMENT TAGS AND TRAITS	What are the traits of avoidant attachment style that you experienced today? Describe how this affected your dealings.
	👍 **WHAT WAS SO COOL:**
	✋ **WHAT WAS WRONG:**

AVOIDANT ATTACHMENT WORKSHEET -DBT-

START YOUR DAY MINDFULLY WITH A FEW MINUTES OF MEDITATION OR MINDFULNESS. THIS PRACTICE WILL HELP YOU FEEL CENTERED, ENHANCE SELF-AWARENESS, AND ESTABLISH A POSITIVE MINDSET FOR THE DAY.

TAKE A MOMENT TO REFLECT ON YOUR EMOTIONS AND EMOTIONAL STATE. ASK YOURSELF ABOUT YOUR FEELINGS, THOUGHTS, AND ANY ATTACHMENT-RELATED PATTERNS YOU MIGHT OBSERVE.

EMBRACE POSITIVE AFFIRMATIONS THAT FOSTER TRUST, VULNERABILITY, AND EMOTIONAL CONNECTION. REPEAT PHRASES LIKE 'I AM DESERVING OF LOVE AND CONNECTION,' 'I AM OPEN TO EMOTIONAL INTIMACY,' OR 'I CAN CONFIDE IN OTHERS WITH MY FEELINGS.'

Mood Tracking

Mood	
ANGRY	☐
ANNOYED	☐
ANXIOUS	☐
ASHAMED	☐
EMBARRASSING	☐
COURAGEOUS	☐
CALM	☐
CHEERFUL	☐
COLD	☐
CONFUSED	☐
DISCOURAGED	☐
DISTRACTED	☐
EMBARRASSED	☐
EXCITED	☐
FRIENDLY	☐
GUILTY	☐
HAPPY	☐
HOPEFUL	☐
SOLITARY	☐
BELOVED	☐
NERVOUS	☐
OFFENDED	☐
AFRAID	☐
THOUGHTFUL	☐
TIRED OUT	☐
UNCOMFORTABLE	☐
UNCERTAIN	☐

Daily Wins

DAILY MOOD CYCLE

Instructions: Think about your day from start to finish. Color the first square to express your feelings each time of the day. Next, write a word that reflects your feelings, and draw in the circle a picture of your face that reflects your feelings at that moment.

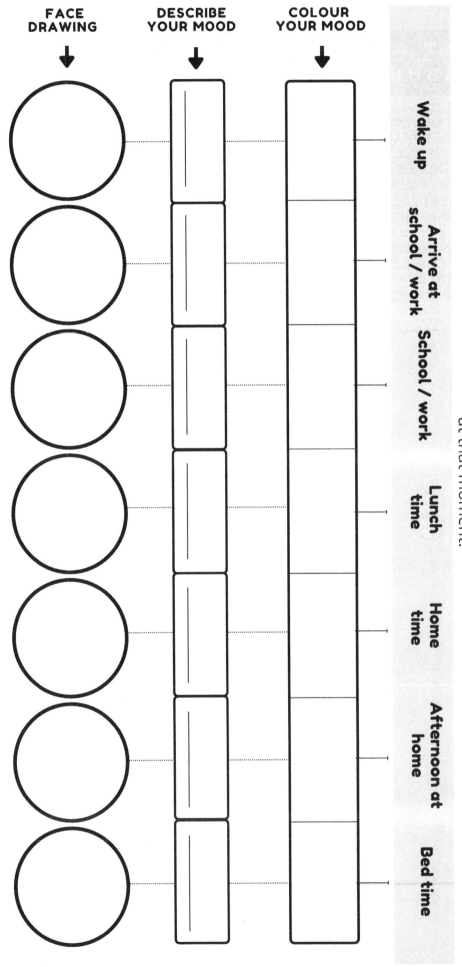

FACE DRAWING

DESCRIBE YOUR MOOD

COLOUR YOUR MOOD

Wake up

Arrive at school / work

School / work

Lunch time

Home time

Afternoon at home

Bed time

AVOIDANT ATTACHMENT WORKSHEET

Date : _____

DAILY / WEEKLY - DBT WORKSHEET (OPTIONAL)

- List three emotions that surfaced throughout yesterday. Reflect on how each emotion affected my interactions and decisions.
- Write a kind and supportive message to myself, focusing on self-acceptance and understanding.
- What are the prospects that will make you give up the difficulty of trusting others and open up.
- Write down one boundary I can set today to prioritize my emotional well-being.
- Write down any lingering worries or thoughts before bedtime, and consider ways to ease them.

Everything related to changing your beliefs about refusing to allow others to approach you for fear of rejection.

_____

_____

_____

_____

_____

_____

_____

_____

_____

_____

_____

_____

_____

_____

_____

DATE :   /   /

EXPOSURE THERAPY
FOR
EMOTIONAL CLOSENESS

Individuals with avoidant attachment may struggle to get close to others, feel unworthy of love and even more so fear getting hurt.

They may avoid emotional intimacy or physical touch, because they see this as threatening.

Start small by engaging in low-risk, casual interactions with others. This could mean saying hello to a neighbor or coworker, or having a brief conversation with a stranger.

Gradually increase the level of intimacy over time.

	TASK ACCOMPLISHED ☐ intimacy level ○ ○ ○ ○ ○
	TASK ACCOMPLISHED ☐ intimacy level ○ ○ ○ ○ ○
	TASK ACCOMPLISHED ☐ intimacy level ○ ○ ○ ○ ○

NOTES

....

....

OVERCOMING AVOIDANT ATTACHMENT WORKSHEET

This table will help you to study the effect of the repercussions of the anxious avoidant attachment style in your social interactions on a daily, weekly or monthly basis... The aim of this paper is to develop an appropriate coping plan to control the negative signs if you want to make a real change in your personality.

AVOIDANT ATTACHMENT TAGS AND TRAITS	What are the traits of avoidant attachment style that you experienced today? Describe how this affected your dealings.
	👍 WHAT WAS SO COOL: ✋ WHAT WAS WRONG:

AVOIDANT ATTACHMENT WORKSHEET -DBT-

START YOUR DAY MINDFULLY WITH A FEW MINUTES OF MEDITATION OR MINDFULNESS. THIS PRACTICE WILL HELP YOU FEEL CENTERED, ENHANCE SELF-AWARENESS, AND ESTABLISH A POSITIVE MINDSET FOR THE DAY.
TAKE A MOMENT TO REFLECT ON YOUR EMOTIONS AND EMOTIONAL STATE. ASK YOURSELF ABOUT YOUR FEELINGS, THOUGHTS, AND ANY ATTACHMENT-RELATED PATTERNS YOU MIGHT OBSERVE.
EMBRACE POSITIVE AFFIRMATIONS THAT FOSTER TRUST, VULNERABILITY, AND EMOTIONAL CONNECTION. REPEAT PHRASES LIKE "I AM DESERVING OF LOVE AND CONNECTION," "I AM OPEN TO EMOTIONAL INTIMACY," OR "I CAN CONFIDE IN OTHERS WITH MY FEELINGS."

⊘ ___ : ___

⊘ ___ : ___

Daily Wins

Mood Tracking ✓

Mood	
ANGRY	☐
ANNOYED	☐
ANXIOUS	☐
ASHAMED	☐
EMBARRASSING	☐
COURAGEOUS	☐
CALM	☐
CHEERFUL	☐
COLD	☐
CONFUSED	☐
DISCOURAGED	☐
DISTRACTED	☐
EMBARRASSED	☐
EXCITED	☐
FRIENDLY	☐
GUILTY	☐
HAPPY	☐
HOPEFUL	☐
SOLITARY	☐
BELOVED	☐
NERVOUS	☐
OFFENDED	☐
AFRAID	☐
THOUGHTFUL	☐
TIRED OUT	☐
UNCOMFORTABLE	☐
UNCERTAIN	☐

DAILY MOOD CYCLE

Instructions: Think about your day from start to finish. Color the first square to express your feelings each time of the day. Next, write a word that reflects your feelings, and draw in the circle a picture of your face that reflects your feelings at that moment.

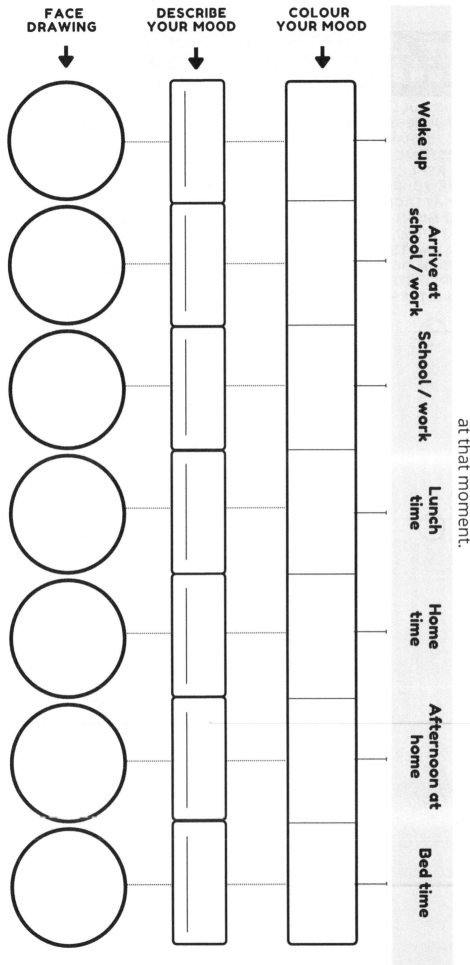

FACE DRAWING

DESCRIBE YOUR MOOD

COLOUR YOUR MOOD

Wake up

Arrive at school / work

School / work

Lunch time

Home time

Afternoon at home

Bed time

AVOIDANT ATTACHMENT WORKSHEET

Date : _____

DAILY / WEEKLY - DBT WORKSHEET (OPTIONAL)

- List three emotions that surfaced throughout yesterday. Reflect on how each emotion affected my interactions and decisions.
- Write a kind and supportive message to myself, focusing on self-acceptance and understanding.
- What are the prospects that will make you give up the difficulty of trusting others and open up.
- Write down one boundary I can set today to prioritize my emotional well-being.
- Write down any lingering worries or thoughts before bedtime, and consider ways to ease them.

Everything related to changing your beliefs about refusing to allow others to approach you for fear of rejection.

_____

_____

_____

_____

_____

_____

_____

_____

_____

_____

_____

_____

_____

_____

_____

DATE :   /   /

EXPOSURE THERAPY
FOR
EMOTIONAL CLOSENESS

Individuals with avoidant attachment may struggle to get close to others, feel unworthy of love and even more so fear getting hurt.

   They may avoid emotional intimacy or physical touch, because they see this as threatening.

Start small by engaging in low-risk, casual interactions with others.

This could mean saying hello to a neighbor or coworker, or having a brief conversation with a stranger.

Gradually increase the level of intimacy over time.

	TASK ACCOMPLISHED ☐ intimacy level ○ ○ ○ ○ ○
	TASK ACCOMPLISHED ☐ intimacy level ○ ○ ○ ○ ○
	TASK ACCOMPLISHED ☐ intimacy level ○ ○ ○ ○ ○

NOTES

....

....

OVERCOMING AVOIDANT ATTACHMENT WORKSHEET

This table will help you to study the effect of the repercussions of the anxious avoidant attachment style in your social interactions on a daily, weekly or monthly basis... The aim of this paper is to develop an appropriate coping plan to control the negative signs if you want to make a real change in your personality.

AVOIDANT ATTACHMENT TAGS AND TRAITS	What are the traits of avoidant attachment style that you experienced today? Describe how this affected your dealings.
	👍 WHAT WAS SO COOL:
	✋ WHAT WAS WRONG:

AVOIDANT ATTACHMENT WORKSHEET -DBT-

START YOUR DAY MINDFULLY WITH A FEW MINUTES OF MEDITATION OR MINDFULNESS. THIS PRACTICE WILL HELP YOU FEEL CENTERED, ENHANCE SELF-AWARENESS, AND ESTABLISH A POSITIVE MINDSET FOR THE DAY.

TAKE A MOMENT TO REFLECT ON YOUR EMOTIONS AND EMOTIONAL STATE. ASK YOURSELF ABOUT YOUR FEELINGS, THOUGHTS, AND ANY ATTACHMENT-RELATED PATTERNS YOU MIGHT OBSERVE.

EMBRACE POSITIVE AFFIRMATIONS THAT FOSTER TRUST, VULNERABILITY, AND EMOTIONAL CONNECTION. REPEAT PHRASES LIKE 'I AM DESERVING OF LOVE AND CONNECTION,' 'I AM OPEN TO EMOTIONAL INTIMACY,' OR 'I CAN CONFIDE IN OTHERS WITH MY FEELINGS.'

☑ ___ : ___

☑ ___ : ___

Daily Wins

Mood Tracking ✓

- ANGRY ☐
- ANNOYED ☐
- ANXIOUS ☐
- ASHAMED ☐
- EMBARRASSING ☐
- COURAGEOUS ☐
- CALM ☐
- CHEERFUL ☐
- COLD ☐
- CONFUSED ☐
- DISCOURAGED ☐
- DISTRACTED ☐
- EMBARRASSED ☐
- EXCITED ☐
- FRIENDLY ☐
- GUILTY ☐
- HAPPY ☐
- HOPEFUL ☐
- SOLITARY ☐
- BELOVED ☐
- NERVOUS ☐
- OFFENDED ☐
- AFRAID ☐
- THOUGHTFUL ☐
- TIRED OUT ☐
- UNCOMFORTABLE ☐
- UNCERTAIN ☐

DAILY MOOD CYCLE

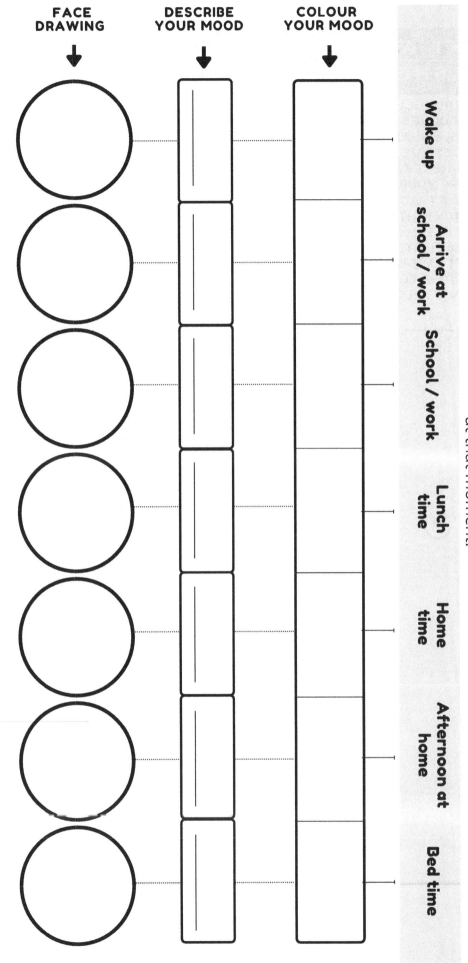

FACE DRAWING

DESCRIBE YOUR MOOD

COLOUR YOUR MOOD

Wake up

Arrive at school / work

School / work

Lunch time

Home time

Afternoon at home

Bed time

AVOIDANT ATTACHMENT WORKSHEET

Date : _____

DAILY / WEEKLY - DBT WORKSHEET (OPTIONAL)

- List three emotions that surfaced throughout yesterday. Reflect on how each emotion affected my interactions and decisions.
- Write a kind and supportive message to myself, focusing on self-acceptance and understanding.
- What are the prospects that will make you give up the difficulty of trusting others and open up.
- Write down one boundary I can set today to prioritize my emotional well-being.
- Write down any lingering worries or thoughts before bedtime, and consider ways to ease them.

Everything related to changing your beliefs about refusing to allow others to approach you for fear of rejection.

_____

_____

_____

_____

_____

_____

_____

_____

_____

_____

_____

_____

_____

_____

DATE :   /   /

EXPOSURE THERAPY
FOR
EMOTIONAL CLOSENESS

Individuals with avoidant attachment may struggle to get close to others, feel unworthy of love and even more so fear getting hurt.

They may avoid emotional intimacy or physical touch, because they see this as threatening.

Start small by engaging in low-risk, casual interactions with others.

This could mean saying hello to a neighbor or coworker, or having a brief conversation with a stranger.

Gradually increase the level of intimacy over time.

	TASK ACCOMPLISHED ☐
	intimacy level ○ ○ ○ ○ ○
	TASK ACCOMPLISHED ☐
	intimacy level ○ ○ ○ ○ ○
	TASK ACCOMPLISHED ☐
	intimacy level ○ ○ ○ ○ ○

NOTES

....

....

OVERCOMING AVOIDANT ATTACHMENT WORKSHEET

This table will help you to study the effect of the repercussions of the anxious avoidant attachment style in your social interactions on a daily, weekly or monthly basis... The aim of this paper is to develop an appropriate coping plan to control the negative signs if you want to make a real change in your personality.

AVOIDANT ATTACHMENT TAGS AND TRAITS	What are the traits of avoidant attachment style that you experienced today? Describe how this affected your dealings.
	👍 WHAT WAS SO COOL: ✋ WHAT WAS WRONG:

AVOIDANT ATTACHMENT WORKSHEET -DBT-

START YOUR DAY MINDFULLY WITH A FEW MINUTES OF MEDITATION OR MINDFULNESS. THIS PRACTICE WILL HELP YOU FEEL CENTERED, ENHANCE SELF-AWARENESS, AND ESTABLISH A POSITIVE MINDSET FOR THE DAY.

TAKE A MOMENT TO REFLECT ON YOUR EMOTIONS AND EMOTIONAL STATE. ASK YOURSELF ABOUT YOUR FEELINGS, THOUGHTS, AND ANY ATTACHMENT-RELATED PATTERNS YOU MIGHT OBSERVE.

EMBRACE POSITIVE AFFIRMATIONS THAT FOSTER TRUST, VULNERABILITY, AND EMOTIONAL CONNECTION. REPEAT PHRASES LIKE 'I AM DESERVING OF LOVE AND CONNECTION,' 'I AM OPEN TO EMOTIONAL INTIMACY,' OR 'I CAN CONFIDE IN OTHERS WITH MY FEELINGS.'

Mood Tracking

- ANGRY ☐
- ANNOYED ☐
- ANXIOUS ☐
- ASHAMED ☐
- EMBARRASSING ☐
- COURAGEOUS ☐
- CALM ☐
- CHEERFUL ☐
- COLD ☐
- CONFUSED ☐
- DISCOURAGED ☐
- DISTRACTED ☐
- EMBARRASSED ☐
- EXCITED ☐
- FRIENDLY ☐
- GUILTY ☐
- HAPPY ☐
- HOPEFUL ☐
- SOLITARY ☐
- BELOVED ☐
- NERVOUS ☐
- OFFENDED ☐
- AFRAID ☐
- THOUGHTFUL ☐
- TIRED OUT ☐
- UNCOMFORTABLE ☐
- UNCERTAIN ☐

Daily Wins

DAILY MOOD CYCLE

Instructions: Think about your day from start to finish. Color the first square to express your feelings each time of the day. Next, write a word that reflects your feelings, and draw in the circle a picture of your face that reflects your feelings at that moment.

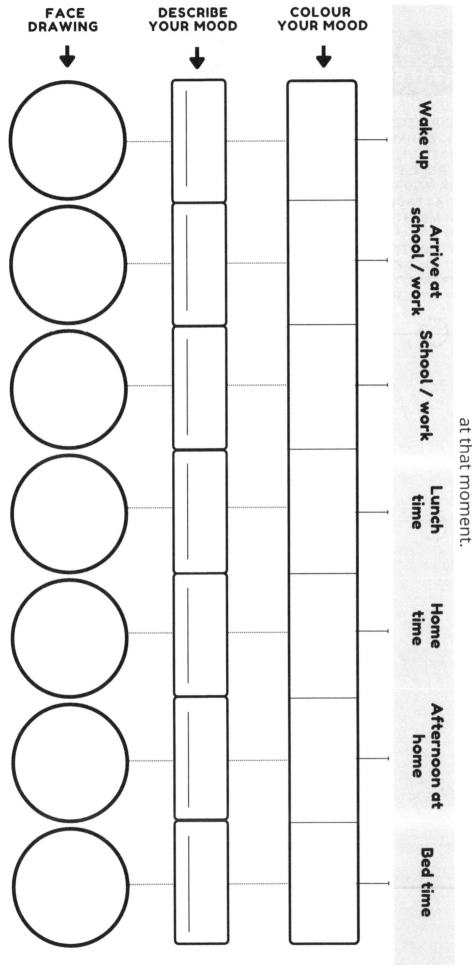

FACE DRAWING

DESCRIBE YOUR MOOD

COLOUR YOUR MOOD

Wake up

Arrive at school / work

School / work

Lunch time

Home time

Afternoon at home

Bed time

AVOIDANT ATTACHMENT WORKSHEET

Date : _____

DAILY / WEEKLY - DBT WORKSHEET (OPTIONAL)

- List three emotions that surfaced throughout yesterday. Reflect on how each emotion affected my interactions and decisions.
- Write a kind and supportive message to myself, focusing on self-acceptance and understanding.
- What are the prospects that will make you give up the difficulty of trusting others and open up.
- Write down one boundary I can set today to prioritize my emotional well-being.
- Write down any lingering worries or thoughts before bedtime, and consider ways to ease them.

Everything related to changing your beliefs about refusing to allow others to approach you for fear of rejection.

EXPOSURE THERAPY FOR EMOTIONAL CLOSENESS

Individuals with avoidant attachment may struggle to get close to others, feel unworthy of love and even more so fear getting hurt.

They may avoid emotional intimacy or physical touch, because they see this as threatening.

Start small by engaging in low-risk, casual interactions with others.

This could mean saying hello to a neighbor or coworker, or having a brief conversation with a stranger.

Gradually increase the level of intimacy over time.

	TASK ACCOMPLISHED ☐ intimacy level ○ ○ ○ ○ ○
	TASK ACCOMPLISHED ☐ intimacy level ○ ○ ○ ○ ○
	TASK ACCOMPLISHED ☐ intimacy level ○ ○ ○ ○ ○

NOTES

....

....

OVERCOMING AVOIDANT ATTACHMENT WORKSHEET

This table will help you to study the effect of the repercussions of the anxious avoidant attachment style in your social interactions on a daily, weekly or monthly basis... The aim of this paper is to develop an appropriate coping plan to control the negative signs if you want to make a real change in your personality.

AVOIDANT ATTACHMENT TAGS AND TRAITS	What are the traits of avoidant attachment style that you experienced today? Describe how this affected your dealings.
	👍 WHAT WAS SO COOL: ✋ WHAT WAS WRONG:

AVOIDANT ATTACHMENT WORKSHEET -DBT-

START YOUR DAY MINDFULLY WITH A FEW MINUTES OF MEDITATION OR MINDFULNESS. THIS PRACTICE WILL HELP YOU FEEL CENTERED, ENHANCE SELF-AWARENESS, AND ESTABLISH A POSITIVE MINDSET FOR THE DAY.

TAKE A MOMENT TO REFLECT ON YOUR EMOTIONS AND EMOTIONAL STATE. ASK YOURSELF ABOUT YOUR FEELINGS, THOUGHTS, AND ANY ATTACHMENT-RELATED PATTERNS YOU MIGHT OBSERVE.

EMBRACE POSITIVE AFFIRMATIONS THAT FOSTER TRUST, VULNERABILITY, AND EMOTIONAL CONNECTION. REPEAT PHRASES LIKE 'I AM DESERVING OF LOVE AND CONNECTION,' 'I AM OPEN TO EMOTIONAL INTIMACY,' OR 'I CAN CONFIDE IN OTHERS WITH MY FEELINGS.'

✓ ___ : ___

✓ ___ : ___

Mood Tracking ✓

- ANGRY ☐
- ANNOYED ☐
- ANXIOUS ☐
- ASHAMED ☐
- EMBARRASSING ☐
- COURAGEOUS ☐
- CALM ☐
- CHEERFUL ☐
- COLD ☐
- CONFUSED ☐
- DISCOURAGED ☐
- DISTRACTED ☐
- EMBARRASSED ☐
- EXCITED ☐
- FRIENDLY ☐
- GUILTY ☐
- HAPPY ☐
- HOPEFUL ☐
- SOLITARY ☐
- BELOVED ☐
- NERVOUS ☐
- OFFENDED ☐
- AFRAID ☐
- THOUGHTFUL ☐
- TIRED OUT ☐
- UNCOMFORTABLE ☐
- UNCERTAIN ☐

Daily Wins

DAILY MOOD CYCLE

Instructions: Think about your day from start to finish. Color the first square to express your feelings each time of the day. Next, write a word that reflects your feelings, and draw in the circle a picture of your face that reflects your feelings at that moment.

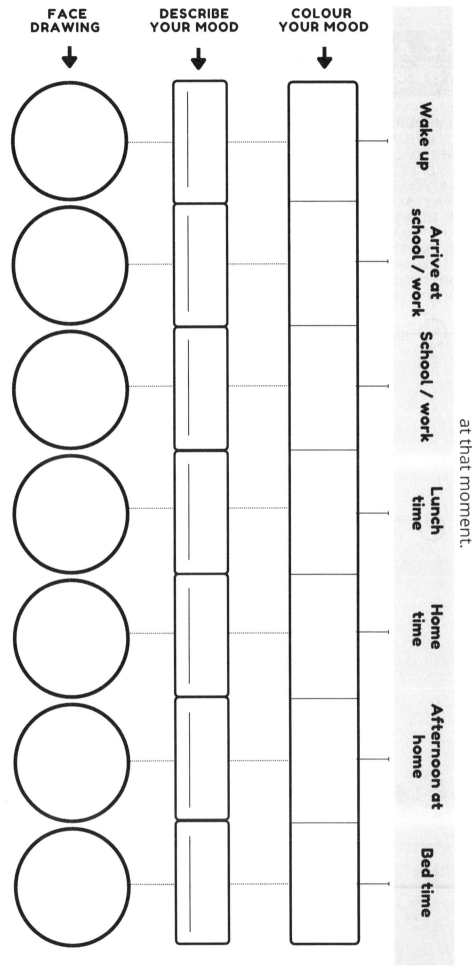

FACE DRAWING

DESCRIBE YOUR MOOD

COLOUR YOUR MOOD

Wake up

Arrive at school / work

School / work

Lunch time

Home time

Afternoon at home

Bed time

AVOIDANT ATTACHMENT WORKSHEET

Date : _____

DAILY / WEEKLY - DBT WORKSHEET (OPTIONAL)

- List three emotions that surfaced throughout yesterday. Reflect on how each emotion affected my interactions and decisions.
- Write a kind and supportive message to myself, focusing on self-acceptance and understanding.
- What are the prospects that will make you give up the difficulty of trusting others and open up.
- Write down one boundary I can set today to prioritize my emotional well-being.
- Write down any lingering worries or thoughts before bedtime, and consider ways to ease them.

Everything related to changing your beliefs about refusing to allow others to approach you for fear of rejection.

_____

_____

_____

_____

_____

_____

_____

_____

_____

_____

_____

_____

_____

_____

_____

DATE :   /   /

EXPOSURE THERAPY
FOR
EMOTIONAL CLOSENESS

Individuals with avoidant attachment may struggle to get close to others, feel unworthy of love and even more so fear getting hurt.

They may avoid emotional intimacy or physical touch, because they see this as threatening.

Start small by engaging in low-risk, casual interactions with others. This could mean saying hello to a neighbor or coworker, or having a brief conversation with a stranger.

Gradually increase the level of intimacy over time.

	TASK ACCOMPLISHED ☐ intimacy level ○ ○ ○ ○ ○
	TASK ACCOMPLISHED ☐ intimacy level ○ ○ ○ ○ ○
	TASK ACCOMPLISHED ☐ intimacy level ○ ○ ○ ○ ○

NOTES

....

....

OVERCOMING AVOIDANT ATTACHMENT WORKSHEET

This table will help you to study the effect of the repercussions of the anxious avoidant attachment style in your social interactions on a daily, weekly or monthly basis... The aim of this paper is to develop an appropriate coping plan to control the negative signs if you want to make a real change in your personality.

AVOIDANT ATTACHMENT TAGS AND TRAITS	What are the traits of avoidant attachment style that you experienced today? Describe how this affected your dealings.
	👍 WHAT WAS SO COOL: ✋ WHAT WAS WRONG:

AVOIDANT ATTACHMENT WORKSHEET -DBT-

START YOUR DAY MINDFULLY WITH A FEW MINUTES OF MEDITATION OR MINDFULNESS. THIS PRACTICE WILL HELP YOU FEEL CENTERED, ENHANCE SELF-AWARENESS, AND ESTABLISH A POSITIVE MINDSET FOR THE DAY.
TAKE A MOMENT TO REFLECT ON YOUR EMOTIONS AND EMOTIONAL STATE. ASK YOURSELF ABOUT YOUR FEELINGS, THOUGHTS, AND ANY ATTACHMENT-RELATED PATTERNS YOU MIGHT OBSERVE.
EMBRACE POSITIVE AFFIRMATIONS THAT FOSTER TRUST, VULNERABILITY, AND EMOTIONAL CONNECTION. REPEAT PHRASES LIKE "I AM DESERVING OF LOVE AND CONNECTION," "I AM OPEN TO EMOTIONAL INTIMACY," OR "I CAN CONFIDE IN OTHERS WITH MY FEELINGS."

✓ ___ : ___

✓ ___ : ___

Daily Wins

Mood Tracking ✓

ANGRY	☐
ANNOYED	☐
ANXIOUS	☐
ASHAMED	☐
EMBARRASSING	☐
COURAGEOUS	☐
CALM	☐
CHEERFUL	☐
COLD	☐
CONFUSED	☐
DISCOURAGED	☐
DISTRACTED	☐
EMBARRASSED	☐
EXCITED	☐
FRIENDLY	☐
GUILTY	☐
HAPPY	☐
HOPEFUL	☐
SOLITARY	☐
BELOVED	☐
NERVOUS	☐
OFFENDED	☐
AFRAID	☐
THOUGHTFUL	☐
TIRED OUT	☐
UNCOMFORTABLE	☐
UNCERTAIN	☐

DAILY MOOD CYCLE

Instructions: Think about your day from start to finish. Color the first square to express your feelings each time of the day. Next, write a word that reflects your feelings, and draw in the circle a picture of your face that reflects your feelings at that moment.

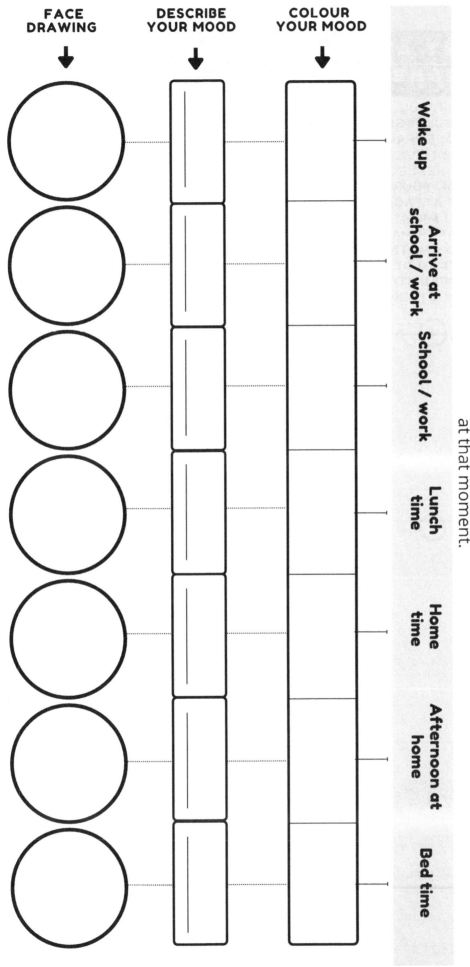

FACE DRAWING

DESCRIBE YOUR MOOD

COLOUR YOUR MOOD

Wake up

Arrive at school / work

School / work

Lunch time

Home time

Afternoon at home

Bed time

AVOIDANT ATTACHMENT WORKSHEET

Date :

DAILY / WEEKLY - DBT WORKSHEET (OPTIONAL)

- List three emotions that surfaced throughout yesterday. Reflect on how each emotion affected my interactions and decisions.
- Write a kind and supportive message to myself, focusing on self-acceptance and understanding.
- What are the prospects that will make you give up the difficulty of trusting others and open up.
- Write down one boundary I can set today to prioritize my emotional well-being.
- Write down any lingering worries or thoughts before bedtime, and consider ways to ease them.

Everything related to changing your beliefs about refusing to allow others to approach you for fear of rejection.

_____

_____

_____

_____

_____

_____

_____

_____

_____

_____

_____

_____

_____

_____

_____

DATE :   /   /

Individuals with avoidant attachment may struggle to get close to others, feel unworthy of love and even more so fear getting hurt.

They may avoid emotional intimacy or physical touch, because they see this as threatening.

Start small by engaging in low-risk, casual interactions with others.

This could mean saying hello to a neighbor or coworker, or having a brief conversation with a stranger.

Gradually increase the level of intimacy over time.

	TASK ACCOMPLISHED ☐ intimacy level ○ ○ ○ ○ ○
	TASK ACCOMPLISHED ☐ intimacy level ○ ○ ○ ○ ○
	TASK ACCOMPLISHED ☐ intimacy level ○ ○ ○ ○ ○

NOTES

....

....

OVERCOMING AVOIDANT ATTACHMENT WORKSHEET

This table will help you to study the effect of the repercussions of the anxious avoidant attachment style in your social interactions on a daily, weekly or monthly basis... The aim of this paper is to develop an appropriate coping plan to control the negative signs if you want to make a real change in your personality.

AVOIDANT ATTACHMENT TAGS AND TRAITS	What are the traits of avoidant attachment style that you experienced today? Describe how this affected your dealings.
	👍 WHAT WAS SO COOL: ✋ WHAT WAS WRONG:

AVOIDANT ATTACHMENT WORKSHEET -DBT-

START YOUR DAY MINDFULLY WITH A FEW MINUTES OF MEDITATION OR MINDFULNESS. THIS PRACTICE WILL HELP YOU FEEL CENTERED, ENHANCE SELF-AWARENESS, AND ESTABLISH A POSITIVE MINDSET FOR THE DAY.

TAKE A MOMENT TO REFLECT ON YOUR EMOTIONS AND EMOTIONAL STATE. ASK YOURSELF ABOUT YOUR FEELINGS, THOUGHTS, AND ANY ATTACHMENT-RELATED PATTERNS YOU MIGHT OBSERVE.

EMBRACE POSITIVE AFFIRMATIONS THAT FOSTER TRUST, VULNERABILITY, AND EMOTIONAL CONNECTION. REPEAT PHRASES LIKE "I AM DESERVING OF LOVE AND CONNECTION," "I AM OPEN TO EMOTIONAL INTIMACY," OR "I CAN CONFIDE IN OTHERS WITH MY FEELINGS."

___ : ___

___ : ___

Daily Wins

Mood Tracking

Mood	
ANGRY	☐
ANNOYED	☐
ANXIOUS	☐
ASHAMED	☐
EMBARRASSING	☐
COURAGEOUS	☐
CALM	☐
CHEERFUL	☐
COLD	☐
CONFUSED	☐
DISCOURAGED	☐
DISTRACTED	☐
EMBARRASSED	☐
EXCITED	☐
FRIENDLY	☐
GUILTY	☐
HAPPY	☐
HOPEFUL	☐
SOLITARY	☐
BELOVED	☐
NERVOUS	☐
OFFENDED	☐
AFRAID	☐
THOUGHTFUL	☐
TIRED OUT	☐
UNCOMFORTABLE	☐
UNCERTAIN	☐

DAILY MOOD CYCLE

Instructions: Think about your day from start to finish. Color the first square to express your feelings each time of the day. Next, write a word that reflects your feelings, and draw in the circle a picture of your face that reflects your feelings at that moment.

FACE DRAWING

DESCRIBE YOUR MOOD

COLOUR YOUR MOOD

Wake up

Arrive at school / work

School / work

Lunch time

Home time

Afternoon at home

Bed time

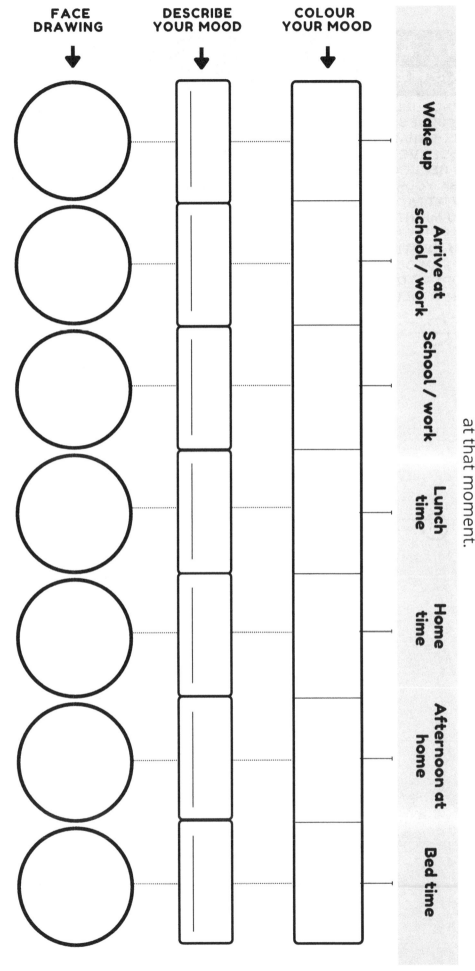

AVOIDANT ATTACHMENT WORKSHEET

Date : _____

DAILY / WEEKLY - DBT WORKSHEET (OPTIONAL)

- List three emotions that surfaced throughout yesterday. Reflect on how each emotion affected my interactions and decisions.
- Write a kind and supportive message to myself, focusing on self-acceptance and understanding.
- What are the prospects that will make you give up the difficulty of trusting others and open up.
- Write down one boundary I can set today to prioritize my emotional well-being.
- Write down any lingering worries or thoughts before bedtime, and consider ways to ease them.

Everything related to changing your beliefs about refusing to allow others to approach you for fear of rejection.

_____

_____

_____

_____

_____

_____

_____

_____

_____

_____

_____

_____

_____

_____

_____

_____

DATE : / /

EXPOSURE THERAPY FOR EMOTIONAL CLOSENESS

Individuals with avoidant attachment may struggle to get close to others, feel unworthy of love and even more so fear getting hurt.

They may avoid emotional intimacy or physical touch, because they see this as threatening.

Start small by engaging in low-risk, casual interactions with others.
This could mean saying hello to a neighbor or coworker, or having a brief conversation with a stranger.

Gradually increase the level of intimacy over time.

	TASK ACCOMPLISHED ☐ intimacy level ◯ ◯ ◯ ◯ ◯
	TASK ACCOMPLISHED ☐ intimacy level ◯ ◯ ◯ ◯ ◯
	TASK ACCOMPLISHED ☐ intimacy level ◯ ◯ ◯ ◯ ◯

NOTES

....

....

OVERCOMING AVOIDANT ATTACHMENT WORKSHEET

This table will help you to study the effect of the repercussions of the anxious avoidant attachment style in your social interactions on a daily, weekly or monthly basis... The aim of this paper is to develop an appropriate coping plan to control the negative signs if you want to make a real change in your personality.

AVOIDANT ATTACHMENT TAGS AND TRAITS	What are the traits of avoidant attachment style that you experienced today? Describe how this affected your dealings.
	👍 WHAT WAS SO COOL: ✋ WHAT WAS WRONG:

AVOIDANT ATTACHMENT WORKSHEET -DBT-

START YOUR DAY MINDFULLY WITH A FEW MINUTES OF MEDITATION OR MINDFULNESS. THIS PRACTICE WILL HELP YOU FEEL CENTERED, ENHANCE SELF-AWARENESS, AND ESTABLISH A POSITIVE MINDSET FOR THE DAY.
TAKE A MOMENT TO REFLECT ON YOUR EMOTIONS AND EMOTIONAL STATE. ASK YOURSELF ABOUT YOUR FEELINGS, THOUGHTS, AND ANY ATTACHMENT-RELATED PATTERNS YOU MIGHT OBSERVE.
EMBRACE POSITIVE AFFIRMATIONS THAT FOSTER TRUST, VULNERABILITY, AND EMOTIONAL CONNECTION. REPEAT PHRASES LIKE "I AM DESERVING OF LOVE AND CONNECTION," "I AM OPEN TO EMOTIONAL INTIMACY," OR "I CAN CONFIDE IN OTHERS WITH MY FEELINGS."

___ : ___

___ : ___

Daily Wins

Mood Tracking ✓

ANGRY	☐
ANNOYED	☐
ANXIOUS	☐
ASHAMED	☐
EMBARRASSING	☐
COURAGEOUS	☐
CALM	☐
CHEERFUL	☐
COLD	☐
CONFUSED	☐
DISCOURAGED	☐
DISTRACTED	☐
EMBARRASSED	☐
EXCITED	☐
FRIENDLY	☐
GUILTY	☐
HAPPY	☐
HOPEFUL	☐
SOLITARY	☐
BELOVED	☐
NERVOUS	☐
OFFENDED	☐
AFRAID	☐
THOUGHTFUL	☐
TIRED OUT	☐
UNCOMFORTABLE	☐
UNCERTAIN	☐

DAILY MOOD CYCLE

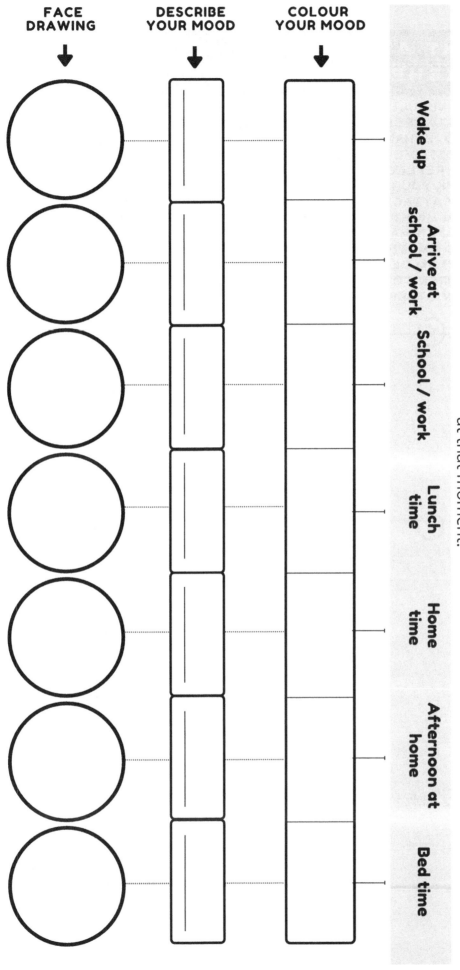

FACE DRAWING

DESCRIBE YOUR MOOD

COLOUR YOUR MOOD

Wake up

Arrive at school / work

School / work

Lunch time

Home time

Afternoon at home

Bed time

AVOIDANT ATTACHMENT WORKSHEET

Date : _____

DAILY / WEEKLY - DBT WORKSHEET (OPTIONAL)

- List three emotions that surfaced throughout yesterday. Reflect on how each emotion affected my interactions and decisions.
- Write a kind and supportive message to myself, focusing on self-acceptance and understanding.
- What are the prospects that will make you give up the difficulty of trusting others and open up.
- Write down one boundary I can set today to prioritize my emotional well-being.
- Write down any lingering worries or thoughts before bedtime, and consider ways to ease them.

Everything related to changing your beliefs about refusing to allow others to approach you for fear of rejection.

_____

_____

_____

_____

_____

_____

_____

_____

_____

_____

_____

_____

_____

_____

_____

_____

DATE :   /   /

EXPOSURE THERAPY FOR EMOTIONAL CLOSENESS

Individuals with avoidant attachment may struggle to get close to others, feel unworthy of love and even more so fear getting hurt.

They may avoid emotional intimacy or physical touch, because they see this as threatening.

Start small by engaging in low-risk, casual interactions with others.

This could mean saying hello to a neighbor or coworker, or having a brief conversation with a stranger.

Gradually increase the level of intimacy over time.

	TASK ACCOMPLISHED □ intimacy level ○ ○ ○ ○ ○
	TASK ACCOMPLISHED □ intimacy level ○ ○ ○ ○ ○
	TASK ACCOMPLISHED □ intimacy level ○ ○ ○ ○ ○

NOTES

....

....

DATE :   /   /

OVERCOMING AVOIDANT ATTACHMENT WORKSHEET

This table will help you to study the effect of the repercussions of the anxious avoidant attachment style in your social interactions on a daily, weekly or monthly basis... The aim of this paper is to develop an appropriate coping plan to control the negative signs if you want to make a real change in your personality.

AVOIDANT ATTACHMENT TAGS AND TRAITS	What are the traits of avoidant attachment style that you experienced today? Describe how this affected your dealings.
	👍 WHAT WAS SO COOL: 🖐 WHAT WAS WRONG:

AVOIDANT ATTACHMENT WORKSHEET -DBT-

START YOUR DAY MINDFULLY WITH A FEW MINUTES OF MEDITATION OR MINDFULNESS. THIS PRACTICE WILL HELP YOU FEEL CENTERED, ENHANCE SELF-AWARENESS, AND ESTABLISH A POSITIVE MINDSET FOR THE DAY.
TAKE A MOMENT TO REFLECT ON YOUR EMOTIONS AND EMOTIONAL STATE. ASK YOURSELF ABOUT YOUR FEELINGS, THOUGHTS, AND ANY ATTACHMENT-RELATED PATTERNS YOU MIGHT OBSERVE.
EMBRACE POSITIVE AFFIRMATIONS THAT FOSTER TRUST, VULNERABILITY, AND EMOTIONAL CONNECTION. REPEAT PHRASES LIKE "I AM DESERVING OF LOVE AND CONNECTION," "I AM OPEN TO EMOTIONAL INTIMACY," OR "I CAN CONFIDE IN OTHERS WITH MY FEELINGS."

Mood Tracking

- ANGRY ☐
- ANNOYED ☐
- ANXIOUS ☐
- ASHAMED ☐
- EMBARRASSING ☐
- COURAGEOUS ☐
- CALM ☐
- CHEERFUL ☐
- COLD ☐
- CONFUSED ☐
- DISCOURAGED ☐
- DISTRACTED ☐
- EMBARRASSED ☐
- EXCITED ☐
- FRIENDLY ☐
- GUILTY ☐
- HAPPY ☐
- HOPEFUL ☐
- SOLITARY ☐
- BELOVED ☐
- NERVOUS ☐
- OFFENDED ☐
- AFRAID ☐
- THOUGHTFUL ☐
- TIRED OUT ☐
- UNCOMFORTABLE ☐
- UNCERTAIN ☐

Daily Wins

DAILY MOOD CYCLE

Instructions: Think about your day from start to finish. Color the first square to express your feelings each time of the day. Next, write a word that reflects your feelings, and draw in the circle a picture of your face that reflects your feelings at that moment.

FACE DRAWING

DESCRIBE YOUR MOOD

COLOUR YOUR MOOD

Wake up

Arrive at school / work

School / work

Lunch time

Home time

Afternoon at home

Bed time

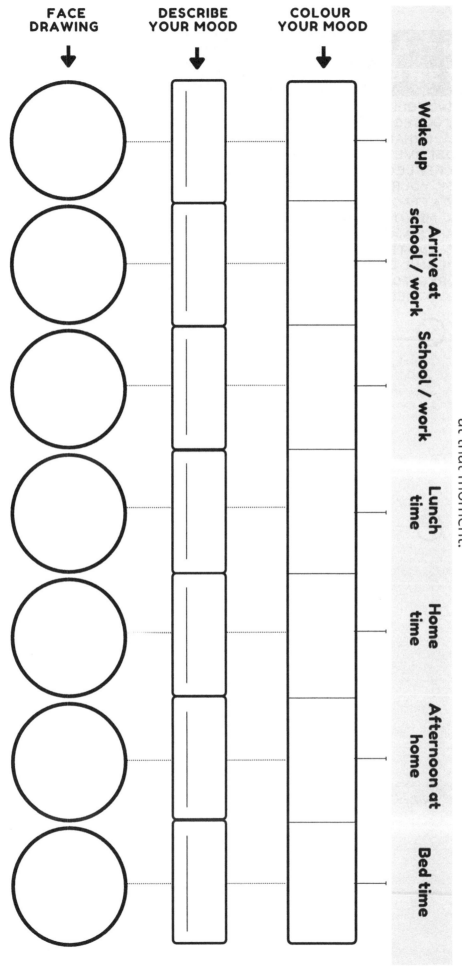

AVOIDANT ATTACHMENT WORKSHEET

Date : _____

DAILY / WEEKLY - DBT WORKSHEET (OPTIONAL)

- List three emotions that surfaced throughout yesterday. Reflect on how each emotion affected my interactions and decisions.
- Write a kind and supportive message to myself, focusing on self-acceptance and understanding.
- What are the prospects that will make you give up the difficulty of trusting others and open up.
- Write down one boundary I can set today to prioritize my emotional well-being.
- Write down any lingering worries or thoughts before bedtime, and consider ways to ease them.

Everything related to changing your beliefs about refusing to allow others to approach you for fear of rejection.

_____

_____

_____

_____

_____

_____

_____

_____

_____

_____

_____

_____

_____

_____

DATE :   /   /

EXPOSURE THERAPY
FOR
EMOTIONAL CLOSENESS

Individuals with avoidant attachment may struggle to get close to others, feel unworthy of love and even more so fear getting hurt.

   They may avoid emotional intimacy or physical touch, because they see this as threatening.

Start small by engaging in low-risk, casual interactions with others.

This could mean saying hello to a neighbor or coworker, or having a brief conversation with a stranger.

Gradually increase the level of intimacy over time.

	TASK ACCOMPLISHED □
	intimacy level ○ ○ ○ ○ ○
	TASK ACCOMPLISHED □
	intimacy level ○ ○ ○ ○ ○
	TASK ACCOMPLISHED □
	intimacy level ○ ○ ○ ○ ○

NOTES

....

....

OVERCOMING AVOIDANT ATTACHMENT WORKSHEET

This table will help you to study the effect of the repercussions of the anxious avoidant attachment style in your social interactions on a daily, weekly or monthly basis... The aim of this paper is to develop an appropriate coping plan to control the negative signs if you want to make a real change in your personality.

AVOIDANT ATTACHMENT TAGS AND TRAITS	What are the traits of avoidant attachment style that you experienced today? Describe how this affected your dealings.
	👍 WHAT WAS SO COOL:
	✋ WHAT WAS WRONG:

AVOIDANT ATTACHMENT WORKSHEET -DBT-

START YOUR DAY MINDFULLY WITH A FEW MINUTES OF MEDITATION OR MINDFULNESS. THIS PRACTICE WILL HELP YOU FEEL CENTERED, ENHANCE SELF-AWARENESS, AND ESTABLISH A POSITIVE MINDSET FOR THE DAY.
TAKE A MOMENT TO REFLECT ON YOUR EMOTIONS AND EMOTIONAL STATE. ASK YOURSELF ABOUT YOUR FEELINGS, THOUGHTS, AND ANY ATTACHMENT-RELATED PATTERNS YOU MIGHT OBSERVE.
EMBRACE POSITIVE AFFIRMATIONS THAT FOSTER TRUST, VULNERABILITY, AND EMOTIONAL CONNECTION. REPEAT PHRASES LIKE "I AM DESERVING OF LOVE AND CONNECTION," "I AM OPEN TO EMOTIONAL INTIMACY," OR "I CAN CONFIDE IN OTHERS WITH MY FEELINGS."

✓ ___ : ___

✓ ___ : ___

Daily Wins

Mood Tracking ✓

- ANGRY ☐
- ANNOYED ☐
- ANXIOUS ☐
- ASHAMED ☐
- EMBARRASSING ☐
- COURAGEOUS ☐
- CALM ☐
- CHEERFUL ☐
- COLD ☐
- CONFUSED ☐
- DISCOURAGED ☐
- DISTRACTED ☐
- EMBARRASSED ☐
- EXCITED ☐
- FRIENDLY ☐
- GUILTY ☐
- HAPPY ☐
- HOPEFUL ☐
- SOLITARY ☐
- BELOVED ☐
- NERVOUS ☐
- OFFENDED ☐
- AFRAID ☐
- THOUGHTFUL ☐
- TIRED OUT ☐
- UNCOMFORTABLE ☐
- UNCERTAIN ☐

DAILY MOOD CYCLE

FACE DRAWING

DESCRIBE YOUR MOOD

COLOUR YOUR MOOD

Wake up

Arrive at school / work

School / work

Lunch time

Home time

Afternoon at home

Bed time

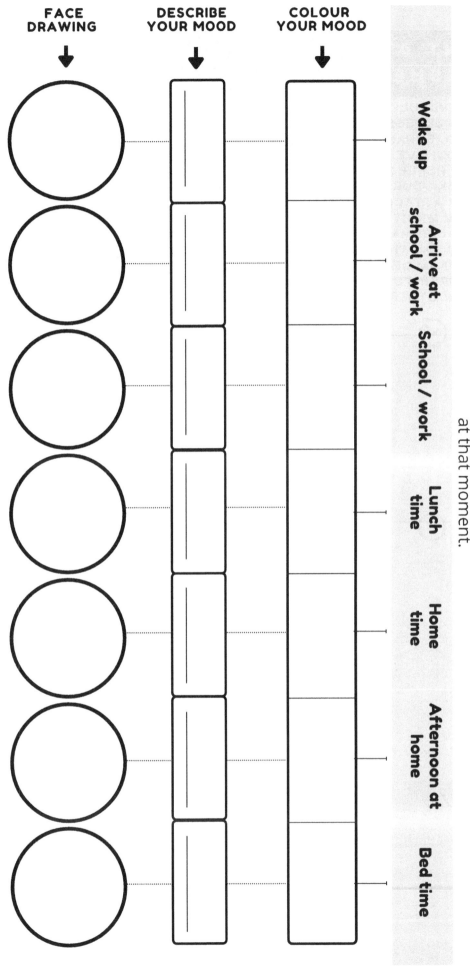

AVOIDANT ATTACHMENT WORKSHEET

Date : _____

DAILY / WEEKLY - DBT WORKSHEET (OPTIONAL)

- List three emotions that surfaced throughout yesterday. Reflect on how each emotion affected my interactions and decisions.
- Write a kind and supportive message to myself, focusing on self-acceptance and understanding.
- What are the prospects that will make you give up the difficulty of trusting others and open up.
- Write down one boundary I can set today to prioritize my emotional well-being.
- Write down any lingering worries or thoughts before bedtime, and consider ways to ease them.

Everything related to changing your beliefs about refusing to allow others to approach you for fear of rejection.

_____

_____

_____

_____

_____

_____

_____

_____

_____

_____

_____

_____

_____

_____

DATE :   /   /

EXPOSURE THERAPY
FOR
EMOTIONAL CLOSENESS

Individuals with avoidant attachment may struggle to get close to others, feel unworthy of love and even more so fear getting hurt.

They may avoid emotional intimacy or physical touch, because they see this as threatening.

Start small by engaging in low-risk, casual interactions with others.

This could mean saying hello to a neighbor or coworker, or having a brief conversation with a stranger.

Gradually increase the level of intimacy over time.

	TASK ACCOMPLISHED ☐ intimacy level ○ ○ ○ ○ ○
	TASK ACCOMPLISHED ☐ intimacy level ○ ○ ○ ○ ○
	TASK ACCOMPLISHED ☐ intimacy level ○ ○ ○ ○ ○

NOTES

....

....

OVERCOMING AVOIDANT ATTACHMENT WORKSHEET

This table will help you to study the effect of the repercussions of the anxious avoidant attachment style in your social interactions on a daily, weekly or monthly basis... The aim of this paper is to develop an appropriate coping plan to control the negative signs if you want to make a real change in your personality.

AVOIDANT ATTACHMENT TAGS AND TRAITS	What are the traits of avoidant attachment style that you experienced today? Describe how this affected your dealings.
	👍 WHAT WAS SO COOL:
	✋ WHAT WAS WRONG:

AVOIDANT ATTACHMENT WORKSHEET -DBT-

START YOUR DAY MINDFULLY WITH A FEW MINUTES OF MEDITATION OR MINDFULNESS. THIS PRACTICE WILL HELP YOU FEEL CENTERED, ENHANCE SELF-AWARENESS, AND ESTABLISH A POSITIVE MINDSET FOR THE DAY.

TAKE A MOMENT TO REFLECT ON YOUR EMOTIONS AND EMOTIONAL STATE. ASK YOURSELF ABOUT YOUR FEELINGS, THOUGHTS, AND ANY ATTACHMENT-RELATED PATTERNS YOU MIGHT OBSERVE.

EMBRACE POSITIVE AFFIRMATIONS THAT FOSTER TRUST, VULNERABILITY, AND EMOTIONAL CONNECTION. REPEAT PHRASES LIKE 'I AM DESERVING OF LOVE AND CONNECTION,' 'I AM OPEN TO EMOTIONAL INTIMACY,' OR 'I CAN CONFIDE IN OTHERS WITH MY FEELINGS.'

✓ __ : __

✓ __ : __

Daily Wins

Mood Tracking ✓

- ANGRY ☐
- ANNOYED ☐
- ANXIOUS ☐
- ASHAMED ☐
- EMBARRASSING ☐
- COURAGEOUS ☐
- CALM ☐
- CHEERFUL ☐
- COLD ☐
- CONFUSED ☐
- DISCOURAGED ☐
- DISTRACTED ☐
- EMBARRASSED ☐
- EXCITED ☐
- FRIENDLY ☐
- GUILTY ☐
- HAPPY ☐
- HOPEFUL ☐
- SOLITARY ☐
- BELOVED ☐
- NERVOUS ☐
- OFFENDED ☐
- AFRAID ☐
- THOUGHTFUL ☐
- TIRED OUT ☐
- UNCOMFORTABLE ☐
- UNCERTAIN ☐

DAILY MOOD CYCLE

Instructions: Think about your day from start to finish. Color the first square to express your feelings each time of the day. Next, write a word that reflects your feelings, and draw in the circle a picture of your face that reflects your feelings at that moment.

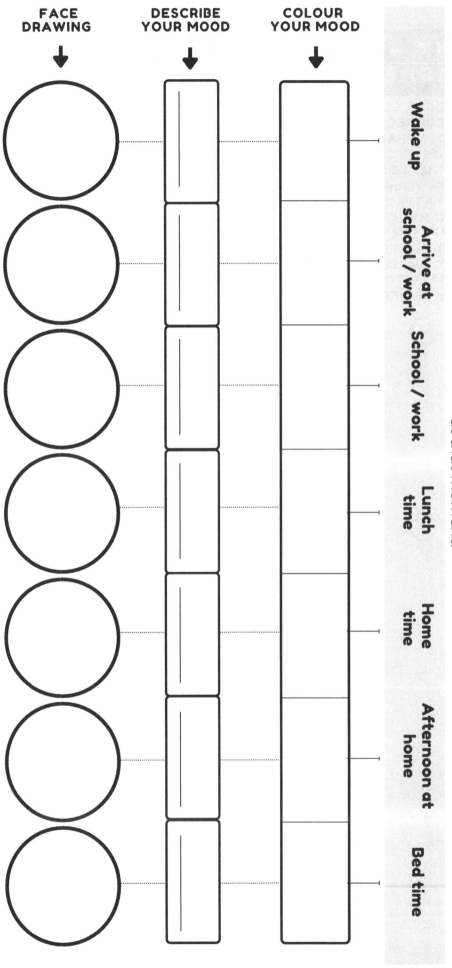

FACE DRAWING

DESCRIBE YOUR MOOD

COLOUR YOUR MOOD

Wake up

Arrive at school / work

School / work

Lunch time

Home time

Afternoon at home

Bed time

AVOIDANT ATTACHMENT WORKSHEET

Date :

DAILY / WEEKLY - DBT WORKSHEET (OPTIONAL)

- List three emotions that surfaced throughout yesterday. Reflect on how each emotion affected my interactions and decisions.
- Write a kind and supportive message to myself, focusing on self-acceptance and understanding.
- What are the prospects that will make you give up the difficulty of trusting others and open up.
- Write down one boundary I can set today to prioritize my emotional well-being.
- Write down any lingering worries or thoughts before bedtime, and consider ways to ease them.

Everything related to changing your beliefs about refusing to allow others to approach you for fear of rejection.

_____

_____

_____

_____

_____

_____

_____

_____

_____

_____

_____

_____

_____

_____

_____

Made in the USA
Monee, IL
28 August 2023

41775281R00059